Lessons on Demand Presents

Teacher Guide and Novel Unit for brown girl dreaming

By:

John Pennington

The lessons on demand series is designed to provide ready to use resources for novel study. In this book you will find key vocabulary, student organizer pages, and assessments.

This guide is divided into two sections. Section one is the teacher section which consists of vocabulary and activities. Section two holds all of the student pages, including assessments and graphic organizers.

Now available! Student Workbooks!

Find them on Amazon.com

Section One

Teacher Pages

Vocabulary

Suggested Activities

NAME:

TEACHER:

Date:

Part 1 Vocabulary

Emancipated

Revolution

Parlor

Bouquet

Scholarship

Memory

Celebration

Part 1 Activities

Reading Check Question / Quiz:

Where do they travel to once leaving Ohio? South Carolina

What did Jaqueline's father want her name to be? Jack

Who was Odella named after? Uncle Odell

Which set of grandparents do the child spend the most time with? Mother's (Gunnar and Georgiana Irby)

Blooms Higher Order Question:

Create a timeline of events for Part One.

Suggested Activity Sheets (see Section Two):

Character Sketch—Jack Austin Woodson

Character Sketch—Mary Anne Irby

Research Connection—Martin Luther King Jr.

Research Connection—John F. Kennedy

Research Connection—Malcom X

Research Connection—Rosa Parks

Research Connection—James Baldwin

Research Connection—Freedom Riders

Compare and Contrast—Ohio vs. South Carolina

Draw the Scene

Who, What, When, Where and How

NAME:

TEACHER:

Date:

Part 2 Vocabulary

Slavery

Amid

Subservient

Inherited

Seamstress

Transformed

Segregated

Paradise

Superstition

Armageddon

Eternity

Infinity

Part 2 Activities

Reading Check Question / Quiz:

For Mary why would home (Parents home) never be the same? Siblings have left.

What name does Jacqueline use for her grandfather? Daddy

When the students had to evacuate Sterling High School, why did they have to attend the elementary school? They were not allowed to attend the white high school.

What religion did the grandmother and children follow? Jehovah Witness

Blooms Higher Order Question:

Create a collage of all the things Jacqueline liked about the South.

Suggested Activity Sheets (see Section Two):

Character Sketch—Gunnar Irby

Character Sketch—Georgiana Scott Irby

Precognition Sheet

What Would You Do?

Poetry Analysis

Poetry Analysis

Poetry Analysis

Discussion Questions

How does Jacqueline feel about the South?

How has the South changed over time?

NAME:

TEACHER:

Date:

Part 3—5 Vocabulary

Constellation

Port

Composition

Immature

Temptation

Brilliance

Disappear

Audience

Resurrection

Mecca

Revolution

Feminist

Chapters 14-27 Activities

Reading Check Question / Quiz:

Why does Roman get sick? From eating paint chips with lead.

What difficulty does Jacqueline have being Odella's younger sister? Odella is smart and teachers expect her to be as smart.

What skill does Jacqueline realize her has? Words/storytelling

What happens with daddy Gunnar? He dies from smoking

Blooms Higher Order Question:

Map all of the locations in the book and trace a string or line in the order they are visited.

Suggested Activity Sheets (see Section Two):

Character Sketch—Jacqueline Amanda Woodson

Character Sketch—Odella Caroline Woodson

Character Sketch—Hope Austin Woodson

Character Sketch—Roman Woodson

Character Sketch— Maria

Character Sketch—Robert Irby

Research Connection—Black Panthers

Create the Test

Interview

Top Ten List—Events

Write a Letter

NAME:
TEACHER:
Date:

Chapter Vocabulary

Chapter Activities

Reading Check Question / Quiz:

Blooms Higher Order Question:

Suggested Activity Sheets (see Section Two):

Discussion Questions

NAME:

TEACHER:

Date:

Chapter Vocabulary

Chapter Activities

Reading Check Question / Quiz:

Blooms Higher Order Question:

Suggested Activity Sheets (see Section Two):

Discussion Questions

Section Two

Student Work Pages

Work Pages

Graphic Organizers

Assessments

Activity Descriptions

Advertisement—Select an item from the text and have the students use text clues to draw an advertisement about that item.

Chapter to Poem—Students select 20 words from the text to write a five line poem with 3 words on each line.

Character Sketch—Students complete the information about a character using text clues.

Comic Strip— Students will create a visual representation of the chapter in a series of drawings.

Compare and Contrast—Select two items to make relationship connections with text support.

Create the Test—have the students use the text to create appropriate test questions.

Draw the Scene—students use text clues to draw a visual representation of the chapter.

Interview— Students design questions you would ask a character in the book and then write that characters response.

Lost Scene—Students use text clues to decide what would happen after a certain place in the story.

Making Connections—students use the text to find two items that are connected and label what kind of relationship connects them.

Precognition Sheet—students envision a character, think about what will happen next, and then determine what the result of that would be.

Activity Descriptions

Pyramid—Students use the text to arrange a series of items in an hierarchy format.

Research Connection—Students use an outside source to learn more about a topic in the text.

Sequencing—students will arrange events in the text in order given a specific context.

Support This! - Students use text to support a specific idea or concept.

Travel Brochure—Students use information in the text to create an informational text about the location

Top Ten List—Students create a list of items ranked from 1 to 10 with a specific theme.

Vocabulary Box—Students explore certain vocabulary words used in the text.

What Would You Do? - Students compare how characters in the text would react and compare that with how they personally would react.

Who, What, When, Where, and How—Students create a series of questions that begin with the following words that are connected to the text.

Write a Letter—Students write a letter to a character in the text.

Activity Descriptions (for scripts and poems)

Add a Character—Students will add a character that does not appear in the scene and create dialog and responses from other characters.

Costume Design—Students will design costumes that are appropriate to the characters in the scene and explain why they chose the design.

Props Needed— Students will make a list of props they believe are needed and justify their choices with text.

Soundtrack! - Students will create a sound track they believe fits the play and justify each song choice.

Stage Directions— Students will decide how the characters should move on, around, or off stage.

Poetry Analysis—Students will determine the plot, theme, setting, subject, tone and important words and phrases.

NAME:

TEACHER:

Date:

Advertisement: Draw an advertisement for the book

NAME:

TEACHER:

Date:

Chapter to Poem

Assignment: Select 20 words found in the chapter to create a poem where each line is 3 words long.

Title:

_____ _____ _____

_____ _____ _____

_____ _____ _____

_____ _____ _____

_____ _____ _____

NAME:

TEACHER:

Date:

Character Sketch

Name

Personality/ Distinguishing marks

Draw a picture

Connections to other characters

Important Actions

NAME:

TEACHER:

Date:

Comic Strip

NAME:

TEACHER:

Date:

Compare and Contrast Venn Diagram

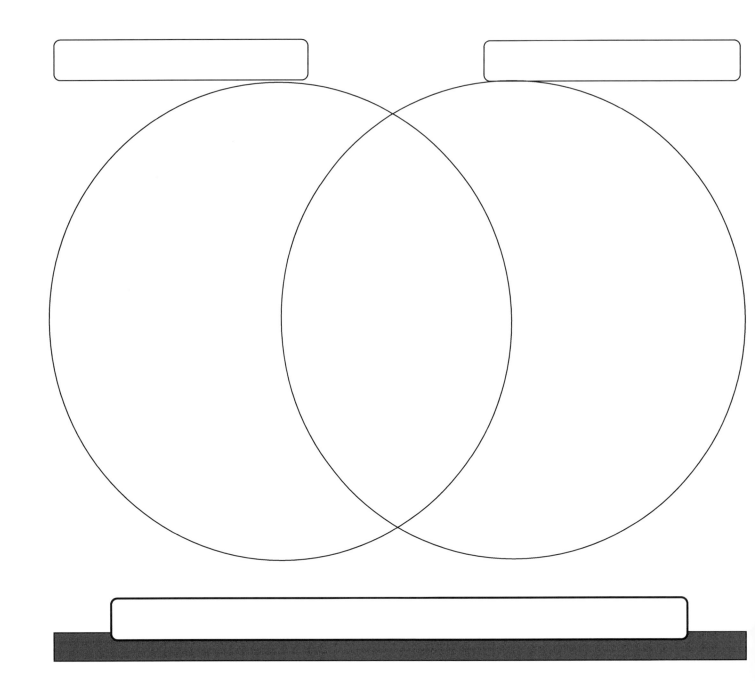

NAME:

TEACHER:

Date:

Create the Test

Question:

Answer:

Question:

Answer:

Question:

Answer:

Question:

Answer:

NAME:

TEACHER:

Date:

Draw the Scene: What five things have you included in the scene?

1   2   3

4   5

NAME:

TEACHER:

Date:

Interview: Who _____

Question:

Answer:

Question:

Answer:

Question:

Answer:

Question:

Answer:

NAME:

TEACHER:

Date:

Lost Scene: Write a scene that takes place between _____ and _____

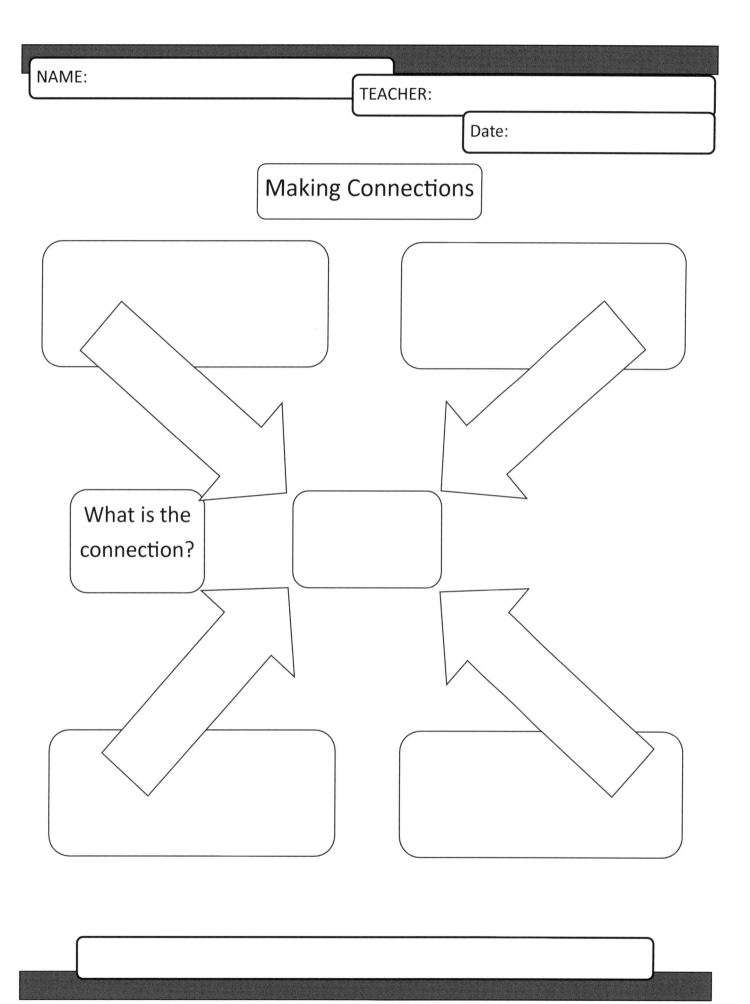

NAME:

TEACHER:

Date:

Precognition Sheet

Who ?

What's going to happen?

What will be the result?

Who ?

What's going to happen?

What will be the result?

Who ?

What's going to happen?

What will be the result?

Who ?

What's going to happen?

What will be the result?

How many did you get correct?

NAME:

TEACHER:

Date:

Assignment: Pyramid

NAME:

NAME:

TEACHER:

Date:

Research connections

Source (URL, Book, Magazine, Interview)

What am I researching?

Facts I found that could be useful or notes

1.

2.

3.

4.

5.

6.

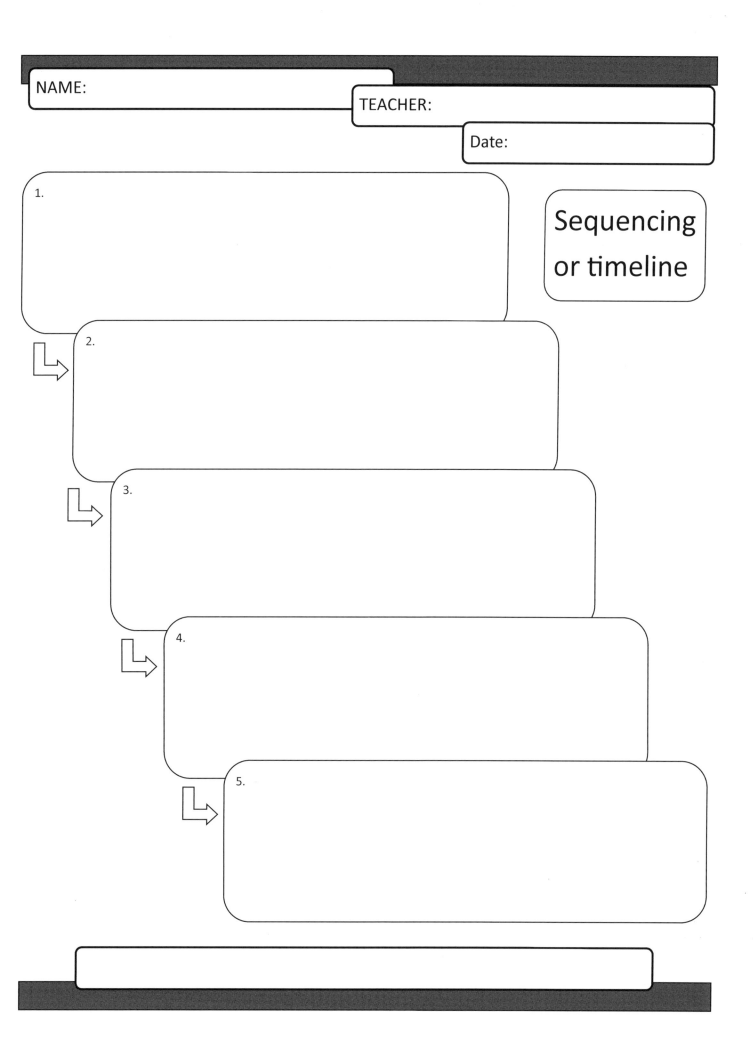

NAME:

TEACHER:

Date:

Support This!

Supporting text

What page?

Supporting text

What page?

Central idea or statement

Supporting text

What page?

Supporting text

What page?

NAME:

TEACHER:

Date:

Travel Brochure

Why should you visit?

What are you going to see?

Map

Special Events

NAME:

TEACHER:

Date:

Top Ten List

1.
2.
3.
4.
5.
6.
7.
8.
9.
10.

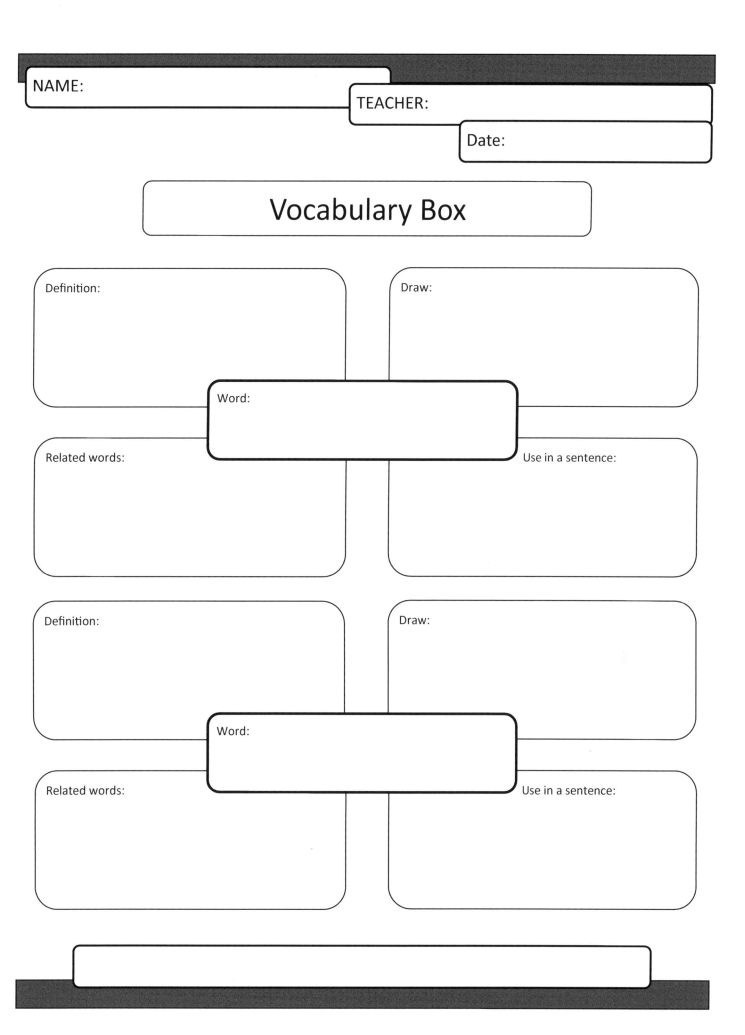

NAME:

TEACHER:

Date:

What would you do?

Character: _____

What did they do?

Example from text:

What would you do?

Why would that be better?

Character: _____

What did they do?

Example from text:

What would you do?

Why would that be better?

Character: _____

What did they do?

Example from text:

What would you do?

Why would that be better?

NAME:

TEACHER:

Date:

Who, What, When, Where, and How

Who

What

Where

When

How

NAME:

TEACHER:

Date:

Write a letter

To:

From:

NAME:

TEACHER:

Date:

Assignment:

NAME:

TEACHER:

Date:

Add a Character

Who is the new character?

What reason does the new character have for being there?

Write a dialog between the new character and characters currently in the scene.

You dialog must be 6 lines or more, and can occur in the beginning, middle or end of the scene.

NAME:

TEACHER:

Date:

Costume Design

Draw a costume for one the characters in the scene.

Why do you believe this character should have a costume like this?

NAME:

TEACHER:

Date:

Props Needed

Prop:

What text from the scene supports this?

Prop:

What text from the scene supports this?

Prop:

What text from the scene supports this?

NAME:

TEACHER:

Date:

Soundtrack!

Song:

Why should this song be used?

Song:

Why should this song be used?

Song:

Why should this song be used?

NAME:

TEACHER:

Date:

Stage Directions

List who is moving, how they are moving and use text from the dialog to determine when they move.

Who:

How:

When:

Who:

How:

When:

Who:

How:

When:

NAME:

TEACHER:

Poetry Analysis

Date:

Name of Poem:

Subject:
- Text Support:

Plot:
- Text Support:

Theme:
- Text Support:

Setting:
- Text Support:

Tone:
- Text Support:

Important Words and Phrases:

Why are these words and phrases important:

Made in the USA
Columbia, SC
12 July 2020